I Got a Boo Boo on My Toe

Poems About Visiting the Pediatrician

by

Michael S. Wolff

Hello, I'm Tallulah
Find me inside!

I Got a Boo Boo on my Toe - Poems About Visiting the Pediatrician

Copyrights © 2019 & 2025 by Michael S. Wolff
doctordoctorseries.com

Published by Gronah Boy Publishing
May 2025

ISBN 979-8-9988844-0-5

Illustrations by Leslie Waara
lesliewaara.com

I would like to thank my wife Amy
For her motivation and encouragement
in the writing of this book.

This book is dedicated to the memory
of
Mary Monica Wolff
(1954 - 1991)

You have an achy stomach
or a boo boo on your toe

Since your Mommy loves you
it's off to the Doc you go

You get to the office
you might feel a little scared

Do not worry because
here are some secrets we will share

A nurse will enter your room
in just a little while

She helps the doc with your care,
so give a big smile

The nurse will take your temperature
and see how much you weigh

When the nurse leaves the room,
tell her to have a nice day

What's the thing around the Doctor's neck?
It looks like a rubber snake

It's just a stethoscope
and your heartbeat it will take

It may feel a little cold
when it first touches your skin

Doc will say breathe out
and then breathe in

Taking your temperature
is something all Doctors do

He can tell if you have a fever
to see what's hurting you

He may ask to put
 a little thing in your ear

it may tickle,
 but do not fear

A thermometer is what he uses
to measure the degree

98 point 6 is normal
a number he'd like to see

To see that you are growing
in just the right way

We measure your height
and see how much you weigh

You step upon a platform,
we slide up some weights

To find out how much
you weigh on this date

Now turn and face forward,
stand up nice and straight

We'll get you height in feet and inches,
Wow you're doing great

Another fun test
the Doctor may try

Is to find out how well
you see from each eye.

You'll cover one eye and look out the other

You'll look at fun shapes
to choose one or another

The shapes might be
letters, squares, circles, or stars

This test will tell if you can see near and see far

A fever is just a number
not an illness by itself

It's just our body saying
it needs a little help

It might be time to get medicine
to give you some protection

To help your body fight off
this thing we call an infection

In our body are tiny cells
that keep out all the bad stuff

They are like little soldiers
tougher than the tough

Sometimes the bad stuff
is stronger than expected

The soldier cells start to lose the battle
and your body becomes infected

When the doctor sees the
little soldiers have lost the fight

He will give you some medicine
to make you feel alright

The Doc just takes a cuff
and wraps it round your arm

Taking your blood pressure
will do you no harm

He then pumps up the cuff
it will start to feel tight

Then he lets it lose
Yay!
You're doing just right

The Doctor has a tool
with a little black tip

To put in your ear
so he can look into it

He'll put his head close
so he can see clear

This will not hurt
no need to fear

The Doc's reflex hammer
has a rubber triangle that *is* round

It's used to test your reflexes
to see that they are sound

A reflex is like when
your leg moves all on it's own

A little tap will make this happen
just below the knee bone

Sometimes the Doctor needs
a little blood from you

Just a quick little sting
and then the job is through

Sometimes from your finger
He may need a little drop

it's not always fun,
but it sure will help a lot

A shot is something
that nobody likes

This is true for parents
and children alike

It's given to you to keep you
from getting real sick

It might hurt for a minute
but it's over real quick

A secret I know
that works pretty fine

Is turn your head away ask,
"What is the time"?

This little tip will keep
the shot off your mind

I'm really proud of you
you're doing just fine

To get a look in your mouth
you must stick out your tongue

We all get to do it
whether old or young

So stick it out straight
and stretch really far,

Ready one-two-three
now give one big AAAAHHHHHH..

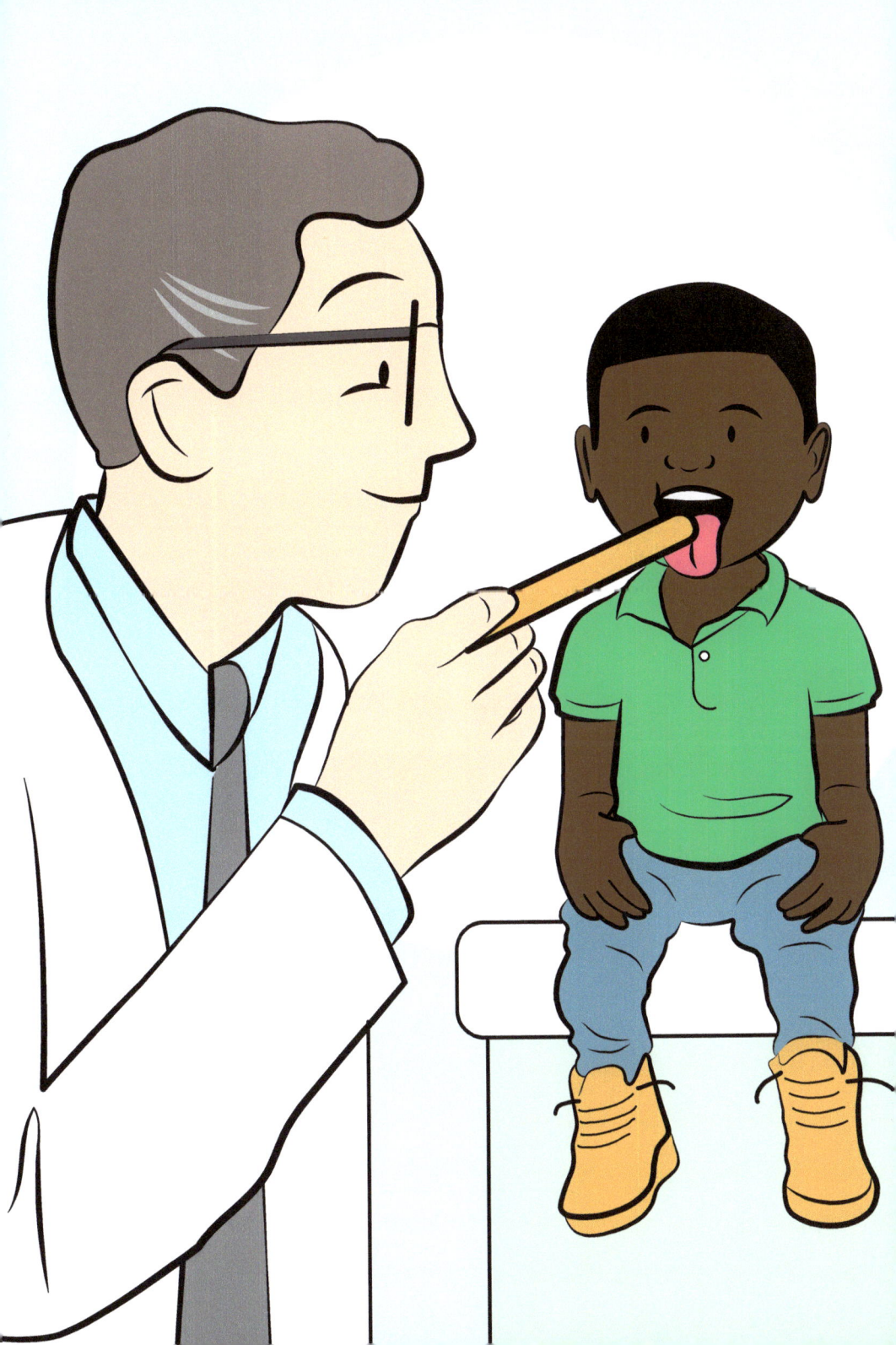

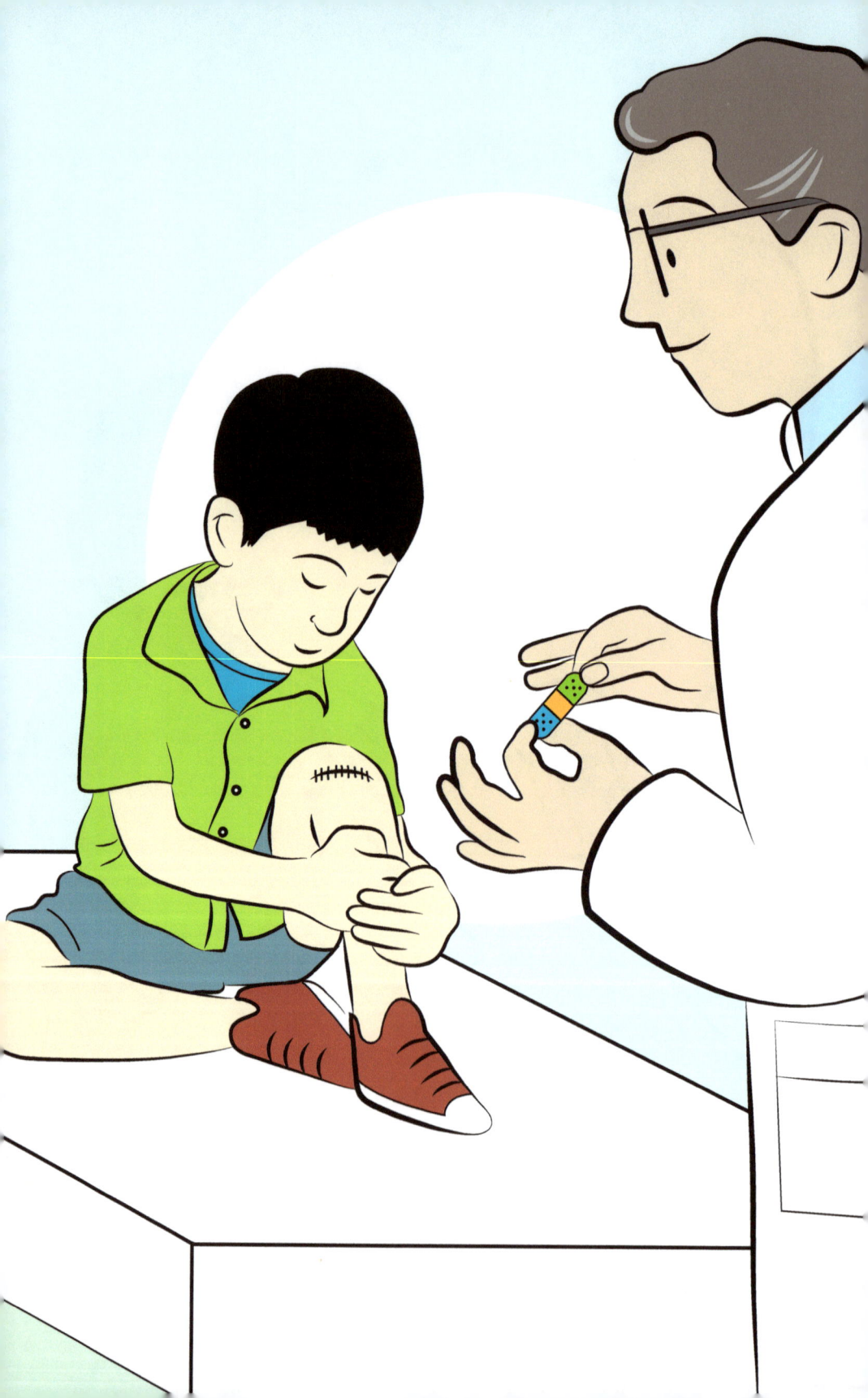

When you cut yourself so deep
a bandage just won't do

You might need some stitches
for it to heal through and through

A Doctor is very careful
using all of his skill

But it is important this time
you sit very still

You might have a scar
it will last more than one day

But after some time
it will probably fade away

Medicine is something to take when you feel funny

It goes in your mouth to get to your tummy

To swallow a pill might be hard to do

But here's a tip for some of you.

Put the pill in your mouth, take a drink, tilt it back

Then swallow it down, you'll soon get the knack

Now liquid medicine is just in a spoon

Swallow it down and you'll feel better soon.

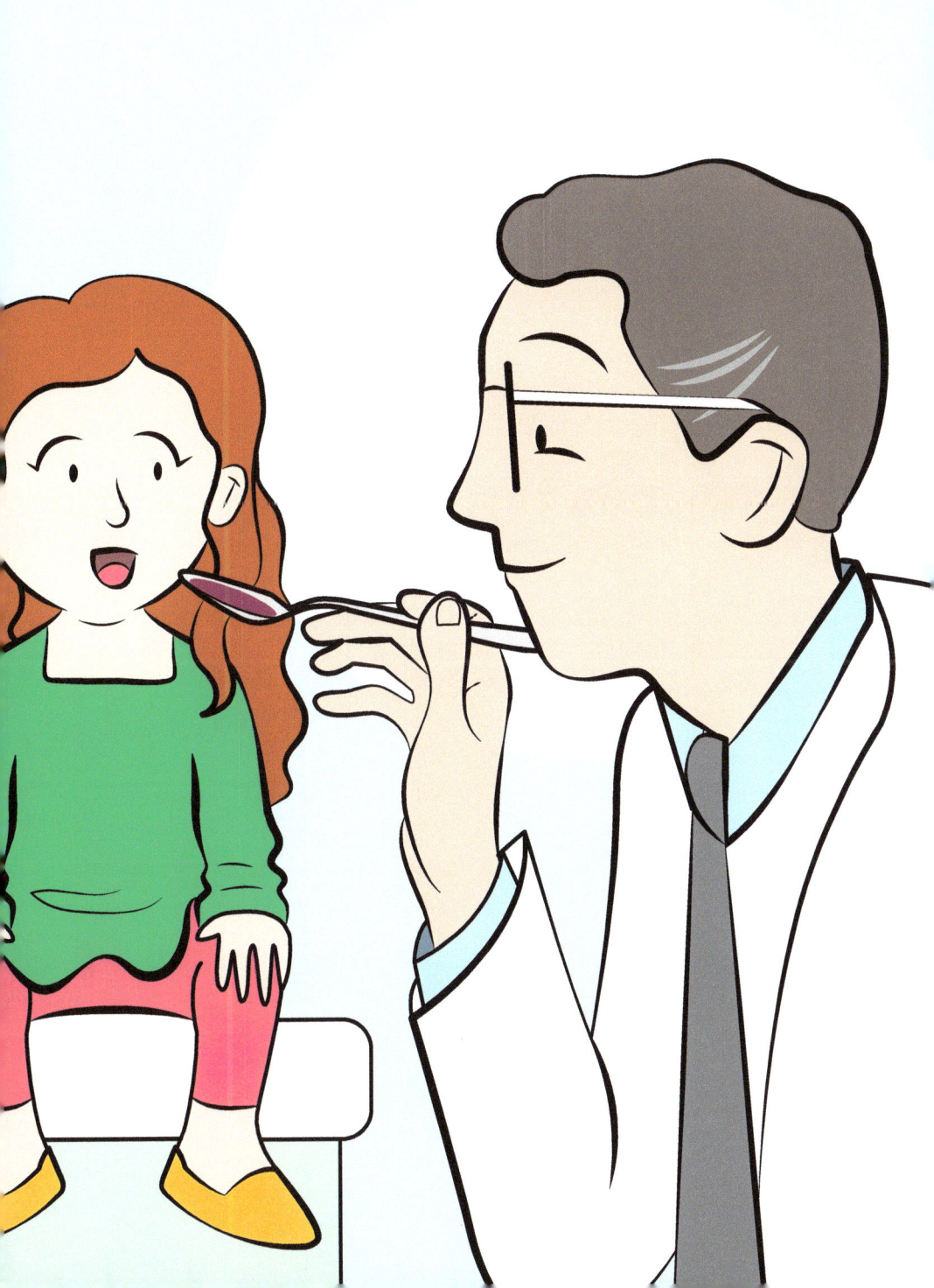

Sometimes while playing
or in the chances you take

You may fall down
and one of your bones may break

The Doc will put it in a splint
or maybe a cast

This protects the bone
and helps it heal fast

If you take it easy
and get it signed by friends

you can go outside
and have fun again

The visit to the Doctor has now come to an end
You now see the Doc's not a bad guy, but is really a friend

All the tests he takes and the things he must do
Are all done to make a healthier you

So as you leave the office give a smile and a wave
Say "Goodbye Doctor and have a nice day"

So until the next time, or when you're feeling really bad
You'll remember this visit and the fun that you had

Now it's your turn

to write a poem about

your friend the doctor

_____

_____

_____

_____

_____

_____

_____

Written by: _____

www.ingramcontent.com/pod-product-compliance
Lightning Source LLC
Chambersburg PA
CBHW040437150626
46551CB00023B/95